ME, MYSELF, AND I CAN

— Your own success story —

JERRY MALDONADO

ISBN 978-1-64028-782-2 (paperback)
ISBN 978-1-64028-783-9 (digital)

Christian Faith Publishing, Inc.
832 Park Avenue
Meadville, PA 16335
www.christianfaithpublishing.com

Printed in the United States of America

DEDICATION

My Olivia,

You are my hero, my strength, and my reason why I work so hard. I devote this to you and all those who suffer in silence. I've watched what makes you happy, and with that, a plan to share with the world.

Love, Daddy

You can become what you think about, or
let what you think about become you.

—Jerry Maldonado

INTRODUCTION

It brings me great pleasure knowing you have something in your hand that can change your life.

The traditional diary is best known as a place of sorrow. Couple this with the pain one carries, and you have an outlet that can lead to a bleak future described in detail. I was spending years writing about the past, which in the end, only created more of it.

Writing is your soul speaking. It brings out your deepest thoughts and feelings that can create a paradise, or living hell. As you read further, you'll get an understanding how to communicate through writing in the most powerful way to the most powerful source. It's what I did to turn my living hell into my paradise.

The Power of the Word

To think (verb) a thought (noun) is a general meaning to create virtually anything out of thin air. To think something is an invisible action that leads to the thought of that something, which in turn creates a feeling. That feeling starts the wheels of evolution in your daily life that can create the noun of your reality.

By writing what you think and feeling that thought, you can create what you set your mind to. It's the general laws of the universe coupled with science that thoughts indeed create things.

Welcome to a New World!

Let me welcome you to a form of manifestation that a few believe in but the most successful use every day.

Some call it scripting, journaling, hypnotic writing, or even verbing (if that's a word); but here's the definition: it's basically a dream board in written form.

Using the think-thought process mentioned previously, you are now going to start a new life. Use these notable instructions below, and you'll attract the miracles that you could only see in your mind but now could hold in your hand.

Here We Go!

How this book works is quite simple yet extremely powerful. You're going to create your future in detail before it even exists. In other words, you're using that think-thought combination to create what you truly want in life. This simple process of using your imagination creates the feeling of this world you desire through writing and with this power sends out energy to start the process.

The action is, when you think so powerfully about what you want continuously with feeling, the natural effects will draw the events, circumstances, and ideas to take physical action on your desires

Passionate continuous thought on anything creates a chemical reaction in the brain, which creates a feeling. You become a magnet with that feeling that attracts into a physical experience to match those feelings. As above (mind, thought, and imagination), so below (reality and feeling from the body, thought, and imagination).

Ironically, everyone does this daily but the wrong way. The repetitive thoughts of lack, frustration, fear, and anger bring about those emotions; and you see how their lives unfold. It's a destructive cycle of many more negative emotions for which there are no happy endings.

Happy beginnings are the result of love, gratitude, forgiveness, and just letting go of who you were to be who you are. Focusing on these and other comparative emotions create a mind full of peace and clarity of focus to begin anew.

There is one important key component to make this work. More concretely, the hardest. You have to believe and have unconditional faith that you can make it happen and live that think-thought feeling every day. You may not know how you can make it happen, but you just know.

This part is where the majority fail. Failure to believe in one's abilities creates doubt, which by definition is a verb. That thought action of repetition only creates more associated feelings, and the snowball effect will continue. The biggest obstacle you will ever endure is thinking. The biggest achievement is the master of self.

This is where my book can help you change everything. It's your personal Bible. It's a place where no one can see. It's your own decree of how you want your life to be. No one can ever change you, except you.

How the Process Begins

To change anything requires you to change your thinking. That's the fact and hard truth. Changing your thinking requires a mental rewire of new thoughts you put in. I did this through affirmations, meditation, writing, and surroundings; but how you do this is up to you. I physically rewrote my new mind-set every chance I could until the new thinking became a natural process. From that transformation, I felt the world was working with me and not against me.

MASTER THIS!

Simply put. Change from there to here. In other words, there is where you want to be. It's your dream or desires fulfilled. It's what you want to happen. It's the outcome of what drives you. Live in the end as it were already here. Feel every word when writing, and you'll begin to see things in your reality change.

You may think this is crazy, or these instructions are from someone who is going out of his mind. Absolutely yes! That's precisely what I'm asking you to do. Look how far you've come in the mind-set you're living? Going out of your mind is a transformation of self to a new mind or a new way of thinking

My Challenge to You!

I believe each of us has something we're born to accomplish or become. It's like being hardwired with a purpose. It's a dream or lifestyle that is so far-fetched in our minds that we could never imagine it happening but comes to mind every day. That's what I'm looking to you to bring out. Create that recurring thought in as much detail and write that thought in as much detail.

Take five minutes each morning and night to dictate that dream or anything you wish to desire or become. Start a routine of thought with feeling about what you want, and you'll notice how these new thoughts expand into other creative thoughts about what it is you want.

Here's a simple trick that can accelerate the process through emotion. Words in written form become an energy force. Take a moment and read what you just wrote out loud with passion. Read as if it already happened and you received it. Once you start adding verbal emotion, you double the energy that is sent out, which eventually returns to you.

Also consider the idea of *not* setting goals. Goals create time limits and pressure you don't need. Most important, this think-thought process is to help rewire your present thinking into daily conscious thought. There should be no time constraints, and goals most likely will only cause frustration that diffuses the process.

Daily write your desires in the most detailed form. Even if it's the same desire every day. The extra effort just but doing this is much more powerful than looking at a list on a piece of paper. Never worry about a time frame to achieve what you want, but write expecting you've received what you want.

Live in the moment is the best advice I can give during this process. Feel those words and try to live in that state of mind as much as you can. It may sound mystical as you can't see it, but this is science evolving that beautiful muscle between your left and right ear to function differently.

Also, this is not a race. Everyone is different at achieving what they wish to bring into their reality. Let go of the concept of time. The gestation period is different for everyone. You can set a target but never a deadline. This method alone alleviates pressure and allows the natural process, coupled with your feelings, to evolve this miracle from out of thin air. You won't be disappointed.

Environment Dictates Outcome

Something to ponder if you're serious about this transformation of self. Like the mental rewire I spoke of, you must consider a physical rewire as well.

The world is filled with beautiful people. The love and compassion we naturally carry is endless, but there is often a catch to receiving such love and it could hinder your chances.

What I've learned on this quest of self is, people mean well but often use others as their own mental punching bag. In other words, they're toxic to what you wish to become. They project out so much negative energy that it actually mentally and physically drains you.

Pick a new environment you wish to have. A place where you can be alone to think clearly. This could be a challenge if your work or family environment is toxic. How you change this situation is up to you, but vital for your personal success. Positive energy cannot feed or transfer to anything off a negative charge.

Most important, your dreams, your desires, and your life should be yours and yours alone. Broadcasting such desires in this social media world puts your vision in the hands of those who have nothing better to do than to mentally destroy them.

SOMETHING TO CONSIDER

Now that you have this book and ready to start anew, I recommend this.

Bad things don't just go away. They're forever ingrained in our subconscious only to be triggered at any point. You can't eliminate them, but you can release them. This whole process takes time, patience, and persistence.

To release anything requires you to accept what has happened and let it go. You've already paid the price for this pain. Forgive yourself and write these words in a separate notepad each day.

"What I manifested that caused pain? I let go."

"The people I hurt? I'm sorry."

"For those who hurt me? I forgive you."

"I am better than this."

"I am worthy to become anything I desire to be."

Write each word as if you're in that situation all over again. Picture yourself smiling as you turn your back after uttering these words and walk away. In time you'll begin to feel peace of mind as you eliminate these daily thoughts and convert to better thinking.

My past is nothing to brag about. I lived through terrible times with vivid memories. I've lost everything twice and rebuilt everything all over, but that's my past, not the future. Scripting created a whole new door of opportunities by realizing the true power I had.

That power was understanding that everything I wanted to manifest comes from the power of thought. Thought is an energy you can't see but feel. That feeling causes emotion that will provide for you the ideas and circumstances to make it happen.

Feeling, coupled with a vision, is a powerful tag team to invoke all the natural laws of the universe to come together on your behalf. Your perception of yourself and the world around you will determine your outcome.

Let's Get Started!

You'll notice each page of this challenge is quite unique. The top part features a few powerful words of encouragement (quotes), while the bottom is my personal commentary to highlight these powerful words. These quotes are a gift that come to me naturally. Use them as motivation in your quest for a new future. You may not understand each one directly, but know they come from the heart and soul of my life experiences.

Use each page as a new day. Begin anew and write accordingly to that new beginning. Most importantly, always keep your writing on a positive level. It may not come out perfect, but time is on your side. Over time you'll notice thoughts about what you want just spring up throughout the day. Use this time to stop and write more, or it will disappear with life's distractions.

I've learned to carry a small notepad to catch my words. Perhaps it's something you should consider if you're really committed to change. Also, I use the alarm on my phone as a reminder. When that alarm goes off, I know it's time to take a minute to focus on my desires.

You Cannot Fail!

It's impossible to fail. When you hyphen impossible you get "im-possible." Keep that thought in mind and understand that if you commit to this think-thought process of living, you'll transform everything in your life.

We all have this gift to use the laws of the universe. Unfortunately, we've been conditioned otherwise. If your life has not turned out the way you thought it would be, it's because of the way you thought it would be. It's that simple. Change how you think about life, and how you think about life will change. It's all about attitude, perception, feeling, and faith, which all of us use but now in a more powerful form that helps create what you truly want.

Much success!

Every day is possible to create the impossible.

What you choose today can be created tomorrow.

Failure is not an option, but a choice.

You choose to fail by not giving yourself the option.

You may not know everything, but
you can create anything.

With the right mind-set, everything falls into place.

When you love life, it loves you back.

Life rewards those who embrace it.

Change how you think, and you'll become that change.

Your choices now will be your reality later.

Karma can be your best friend or worst enemy.

What you wish upon you, brings upon.

Move forward with your thoughts, and
not backward with your memories.

What you live in now will be created later.

You can follow someone or become someone.

There can be no light living in the shadow of others.

There are no limits to a limitless mind.

Create a limitless vision, and live in it.

Don't become what you think about;
become what you dream about.

Bring that dream to life by dictating it.

Every chance is an opportunity to give yourself one.

More chances will offer more opportunities.

If you dream, you create. If you dwell, you destroy.

What you create is up to you.

Forgiveness is a gift you give yourself.

The path to change is learning to let go
of what you're trying to change.

Give yourself a future by not living in the past.

Learn from the past, so you can create an amazing future.

The light can only shine if you decide to let it.

Once you let go of darkness, the sun will shine again.

Life is not one's substance of success, but of significance.

It's what you feel about success, and
not what you attain as a result.

Stress takes a toll on the soul.

Stress blocks the creativity that can help you
become that person you wish to be.

What you think about now can become your reality later.

Change your thoughts, and you change your life.

To know what you want will get you what you want.

With a vision comes happiness.

You are going through something to become something.

Bad things happen that will often lead
to good things happening.

Those with the most opinions have the least results.

You never learn from a one-sided mind.

A hug is rarely offered, but always needed.

Those who've fallen hard can be lifted by this simple gesture.

Anything is possible to those who think it's possible.

Nothing is impossible to a limitless mind.

Stop talking about your dream, and start becoming it.

You create a path not by the words you
speak, but the steps you take.

Strive to thrive.

Keep trying to be something, and you'll be rewarded by becoming something.

Find your passion, and you'll find your purpose.

Happiness in what you're doing is passion in action.

Happiness is a choice, so is misery.

Consider happiness the gift you give yourself.

Don't prove yourself, just be yourself.

Never a need to explain wholeness, if
you are content with yourself.

Age is not a number, but an attribute of wisdom.

Embrace age as the knowledge needed
to get to the next level.

True happiness is found when you
let the true you come out.

It takes tremendous courage to step
out, but the rewards are endless.

There is a reason for everything and
an answer in everything.

Learn from mistakes, and be rewarded in the future.

When you love life, it loves you back.

Karma will always have your back on this.

Success is not by chance, but by choice.

Whatever you choose in life, you become in life.

Change your mind, and you change your life.

All change start with the decision to do so.

Your thoughts are the preamble to your future.

You write the story with thought,
and finish it with action.

When you start believing, you start achieving.

This is the mind-set of success.

Those who say you can't most likely have done nothing.

Surround yourself with those who encourage
you and not discourage you.

Believe in who you are, and you'll
become who you wish to be.

Nothing can stop a person with a purpose.

Desire brings all things desired.

Your inner desire to become better is
the beginning to be better.

Blunt words have sharp edges.

Words have the power to inspire or destroy.

Not only can your eyes see things,
but project them as well.

Use imagination to project out what
you want and not what you see.

What you give energy, too, becomes a part of you.

Focus is energy you put out that over time
will become a reality in your life.

You go through something to become something.

Every ending has a new beginning.

Your purpose is to become your purpose.

Life will change when you realize why you're here.

Most know a lot, but fail to do a lot.

Everything will fall into place for those who have the courage and take that first step.

You are what you say you are.

Dictate what inspires you, and continue
that mantra as a lifestyle.

One change will change everything.

One step will always lead to another.

Thoughts now become things later.

Just the thought of change starts the process of it.

Never try to be someone, only become someone.

You'll never feel true happiness until you create your own.

Sometimes, it takes us to fall hard in order to stand tall.

There is a reason why things happen, and
a bigger reason to overcome it.

Failure is not taking a chance, but giving yourself one.

Every chance you take is an opportunity to be great.

Stop trying to fit in, and start trying to stand out.

The only person you can truly be is the
person you have the courage to be.

You'll never find a happy place
surrounded by negative people.

You can change that by changing your environment.

There are no limits except those you create.

If you can illustrate your limits, you can
illustrate a plan to overcome those limits.

Fear is taught by others who live in it.

Your life now was shaped by the
thoughts and beliefs of others.

Dwell on what you can do instead of can't do.

You create your own barriers, and build your own doors.

With a vision comes happiness.

Illustrate with clarity, and watch the world help create it.

What you see now, you can be later.

Imagination offers a vision to what
you can become in advance.

Your words are the compass to the future.

Success is an emotion that guides to future success.

Never question yourself, just be yourself.

Trust who you are, and you'll become who you wish to be.

"Be your own special kind of beautiful."

One of my favorite quotes that changed my life.

Love what you do, and you'll attract
the right things to you.

Love will always lead the way to more of it.

When you can freely express yourself, you can be yourself.

That is expression without concern or guilt.

The past is not to live by, but to learn from.

Every painful lesson can create a pleasurable future.

Small minds judge many.

A small mind will bring small results.

Think about what you're thinking about.

Your future depends on what you're thinking now.

There are those who act the part,
and those who become it.

Your dream will become real when you
move into the thought of it.

When you keep telling it like it is,
you will keep it like it is.

Limited thinking creates a limited outcome.

Good things come when you let the bad things go.

Let go of the past, so the future can come in.

Wholeness brings happiness.

Wholeness is just being you without reservation.

The courage to do something is your
purpose to become something.

The hardest step is the first one.

Time doesn't heal old wounds, only you can.

Peace will come when you decide to let it in.

When your dreams become your life,
your life becomes your dream.

Dictate what you want, and the world responds.

Be yourself or be nothing.

The world is yours with this conviction.

The smallest steps create the biggest rewards.

One step will create more steps.

When you take a chance, you give yourself a chance.

From failure comes opportunity.

There are no limits to a limitless mind.

A limitless mind carries limitless opportunities.

Your highest thought is the foundation
of your future reality.

It is what you believe in that you will be shaped from.

You have the choice to follow something
or become something.

Follow your bliss, and more of it will come to you.

Stop doubting who you are so you can
become who you want to be.

When you doubt yourself, you limit yourself.

You have a choice to change the world,
or the world will change you.

The world is your current surrounding that
may send you in the wrong direction.

You can get busy doing, or die doing nothing.

The graveyard is a monument to those who've never tried.

When you truly believe in yourself, you'll become yourself.

The courage to be stems from the
conviction that you can be.

It's not by chance you succeed, it's by choice.

When you make the choice, you give yourself a chance.

Your day will be determined by your idea about it.

You wake up with a chance. You determine it by choice.

Never prove yourself, just be yourself.

Prove to yourself to be yourself.

Judge no one, as you may become that someone.

Wasting your time to judge is a loss of time to succeed.

Success doesn't happen to you, but is created by you.

You create the circumstances by the actions you take.

Turn off the world around you, and
turn on what's inside you.

Focus not on what's happening, but
what you can make happen.

A future begins with a new mind-set.

A mind-set is the foundation that
starts the process for change.

You are what you say you are.

Every word you speak of you eventually bring of.

How you feel about life is what you get from it.

Use karma for you, instead of against you.

Your thoughts of the past will be eliminated
with a vision for the future.

A powerful dream will put the past to rest.

What you settle for now, you'll regret later.

You deserve everything, and should
never settle for anything.

The world will tell you how to be, but only
you decide who you want to be.

Following others most likely will lead you to nowhere.

When you expect nothing, you get nothing.

Expectation will bring you exactly what you're expecting.

Inside everyone is the desire to become someone.

You have a vision, and the choice to create that vision.

Stop dwelling on what happened, and start
creating what you can make happen.

The past happened. The future you make will happen.

You need a job to survive, but a dream to live.

Be thankful for the job and be blessed you have a dream.

You can shape your future reality by your
thoughts of the present reality.

Dictate how you feel to see if it matches
with what you wish to create.

Faith is not taking a chance, but giving yourself one.

You never lose when you believe in yourself.

Your mouth can be a shovel to dig your own grave.

Speak wisely in a world full of ignorance.

Misery loves company, but happiness is one thought away.

You can focus what helps, or dwell on what hurts.

Our legacy is not what we leave, but what we teach.

Wisdom never carries a price tag.

Every minute you hold onto the past is
less you have to enjoy the future.

Use time to focus on what moves you
forward and not hold you back.

Focus not on what you don't have, but what you will have.

You have this choice in life to see the
future before it happens.

You must believe in yourself to become yourself.

Faith is confidence and the driving force.

If God can forgive, why can't you?

Forgiveness is the gift you give yourself.

Don't insult others' faults, but praise their attributes.

Look at the person and not the problems.

Your children will thank you later for being here today.

A child's future is a reflection on who raised them.

We all have the will, but only a few have the courage.

The will is your passion to overcome
anything in order to be something.

Those who quit never win, while those who don't always do.

You never lose if you try, but you must keep trying in order to never lose.

Either teach your children, or someone else will.

Show your children the right way, or someone else may show them the wrong way.

You may not have a lot, but you can certainly give a lot.

People don't need charity but inspiration.

Stop telling your children what they can't accomplish,
and start telling them what they can accomplish.

Encourage them, not discourage them.

Don't teach what you can't follow.

Hypocrisy will underscore your character in life.

Life will only give up on those who give up on life.

Life will give everything you speak of or ask for.

Not only are we blessed with life,
but the gift to change it—

Powerful, choice words we all should live by.

Think not of those who hurt you, but who've helped you.

Focus on those who ran into the fire, as others fled.

Your past will always call, but it's your choice to answer.

Live in the moment instead of the memory.

You can't change where you've been,
but you can where you're going.

Move forward with your thoughts, and
not backward with your memories.

Your eyes see the world, but your mind can see the future.

Imagination can be your future reality shown in advance.

You can't allow others in until you let others out.

Clean house of negativity, and provide
a welcome mat to live positively.

You will always have a chance, if you give yourself one.

Never give up on who you are and
who you wish to become.

What makes the man is not what he
attained, but how he attained it.

Enjoy the path to become something better.

Our biggest enemy is not the outside
world, but our inside world.

What we perceive most likely is what we believe.

Before you judge, look in the mirror.

How you judge others now is how you'll be judged later.

Dreams don't die, only one's passion to attain it.

Fuel that dream with passion, and
watch the magic happen.

The only limits in life are what you think of.

A limitless mind offers unlimited opportunities.

Emotions may break the heart, but
words lacerate the soul.

Every word has meaning, and can
destroy a mind-set instantly.

A good deed should not be for attention,
but for giving attention.

Do good because you want to, not because you have to.

The bridges you burn may need to be crossed someday.

Those you hurt may be needed someday.

Some will predict your future, but only you can dictate it.

Surround yourself with doers instead of doubters.

Some will laugh at your situation, but
you will laugh at the outcome.

Revenge is sweet, but success is sweeter.

Your past may hold secrets, but your
future can hold promise.

Your future depends on your ability to focus on it.

You can put a question mark on why things happen, or add a period and begin again.

It's hard to let things go, but is a necessity to grow.

There is always a job for the pessimist,
and a dream for the optimist.

You can be like everyone, or step
up and become someone.

Your dreams are only irrelevant to those
who don't believe in them.

You bring dreams to life by believing you can do so.

The past only comes to life when you give it life.

What you focus on, brings upon.

Hatred never affects the target, but
only those who pull the trigger.

Those who hate suffer more than those who are hated.

Selfishly is not how you live, but telling others how to live.

Live your life, and let others attain their own.

Happiness is a choice, so is misery.

Start each day with that simple choice.

Facts don't lie, theories do.

Find the truth and you'll find peace.

Failure is nothing more than a chance to get it right.

Success is guaranteed to those who
believe in these simple words.

Those who doubt themselves will always doubt others.

You won't receive positive information
surrounded by negative people.

People will always jump onboard
when your ship stops sinking.

Beware of those who disappear, only to reappear.

If you're looking for a miracle, look in the mirror.

In that reflection is someone truly special.

You can sit back and do nothing, or change
your mind and become something.

It's in decision to change is when things happen.

Give yourself a future by not living in the past.

Overcome what haunts you, and
welcome what inspires you.

We are born into love, but taught to hate.

The environment shapes us until we
understand how to change the mold.

People will judge by where you are
instead of where you're going.

No need to prove anything to those
most likely won't listen.

Nothing you achieve is more important
than the person you become.

Enjoy the process knowing where you're going.

Sometimes you need to go through something
bad to become something better.

In these events, you find out how strong you truly are.

Faith is your soul speaking.

As you listen, so shall you become.

Your past is not to live by, but to learn from.

We all learn something by going through something.

With a vision comes happiness.

A vision is a purpose you've constructed before
it's built with assurance that it's coming.

What you say today, you could become tomorrow.

Always speak in a positive light, and
you'll attract more sunshine.

Be your own special kind of you.

Welcome that person you see inside
that wants to come outside.

Courage opens new doors and closes old ones.

You hold the key to all opportunities.

Faith creates ideas. Hope wishes for them.

Faith is clarity that helps create better solutions.

Happiness is choosing to be happy;

A simple choice that will change everything around you.

The majority spend their time
impressing instead of expressing.

Just being who you're happy being will
alleviate any insecurities you may have.

You'll attract exactly what you think of you—

A scientific fact that few understand,
but so simple to follow.

Once you let go of tomorrow, you can begin to live today.

Moving forward can never be attained
with backward thinking.

Fear is a choice that will only lead to more of it.

Fear is an emotion that stops you from
being what you're trying to be.

True beauty is not what you see, but what you feel.

Sounds backward, but true inner power is
attained when you understand this.

Enjoy the moment instead of the memory.

Live for now, so you can create an amazing experience.

You make a difference not by who you
are, but who you've become.

Your legacy will be measured by how
many hearts you've touched.

True happiness is being who you are not afraid of being.

Amazing courage brings amazing rewards.

How you speak of others is most likely
how you think of yourself.

Your character is always transparent to the outside world.

If the past hurts, go create a new one.

You have the power to create any
past you wish to visit again.

When you truly believe in yourself,
you'll believe in others.

It always starts with how you feel about you.

You can follow someone, or become someone.

Dictate who you wish to become, and read
out loud those words every day.

Look inside for answers, and you'll find them.

The mind will lead the way, if you ask for direction.

When you stop dwelling, you start creating.

You choose the time to overcome, and you choose the time to move forward.

Inside everyone is the desire to become someone.

We all have something to share, and
with courage comes happiness.

When you expect nothing, you get nothing.

When I changed my attitude, I changed my life.

How you feel about life is exactly what you get from it.

When you give life a chance, you'll be given a chance.

Don't look back on who you were for
who you wish to become.

Things happen, and we're blessed to
make better things happen as well.

The truth never needs explanation.

An honest heart will always sleep in peace.

Stop complaining and start creating.

What you give attention to will be attracted to you.

Faith in your abilities will always create possibilities.

Believe in what you can become, and it will happen.

You are not what others say, but how you think.

What others think of you has no meaning
compared to how you think of yourself.

Imagination is creating your future reality.

Live by this rule of life, and everything
you've asked for will become.

Before you create that person outside, you
must become that person inside.

Success is a mind-set way before a lifestyle.

Never prove yourself, just be yourself.

You'll never shed light to blind eyes.

Your attitude determines your outcome.

What you truly believe in, you'll become.

You can sit around and do nothing, or
step up to become something.

Wipe away the tears of disappointment,
and create tears of joy.

Some will try to write your story, but
only you can finish the book.

Don't share your shoes with those
who wish to walk in them.

Imagination is creation before creation.

Sounds crazy, but true.

You have a choice to change the world,
or the world will change you.

You can truly be something the world needs,
or something the world destroys.

Live with the past behind you instead of in front of you.

A powerful form of living with amazing rewards.

When you doubt nothing, you can change anything.

Dictate those doubts, and know you have
all that is needed to overcome them.

You have a choice to follow a trend or create one.

In the shadow of others lies nothing but darkness.

If it doesn't feel right, it will never turn out right.

Trust your judgment, and believe what you feel.

Focus not what happened today, but
what you can create tomorrow.

It's a powerful choice of thought
that can change everything.

Start each day looking forward instead of backward.

With a vision, you'll never have this problem.

The smallest steps create the biggest rewards.

I'm sure you've heard of this, but are you doing this?

It's okay to fail, but not okay to quit.

Unrelenting effort will take your
cause, and bless your effect.

What you surround yourself with, you'll become.

Illustrate your environment in great detail,
and see if it matches your vision.

When you take a chance, you give yourself one.

Every chance leads to opportunity.

People like change, not being changed.

You decide who you want to become, and
not become what others want.

You are what you say you are.

Every word you speak is a reflection of how you feel.

How you see yourself is how the world responds.

The world will give you exactly what you believe in.

Success doesn't happen to you, but is created by you.

Everything came together when I adopted this belief.

When you make a difference, you
help others make a difference.

Your creation helps others come up
with their own creation.

The thoughts you carry can move you
forward or take you back.

With a vision comes thoughts that help create that vision.

Those with the most opinions have the least results.

Opinions show the character of the
person who voices one.

People leave us to allow others to find us—

A great perspective to live by when things happen.

You deserve a future, and the future deserves you.

Give yourself credit that you are here to become something really big.

If you can't express yourself, you can't be yourself.

Happiness is never attained from living two lives.

What you follow is what you become.

Think about what you've followed,
and where has it lead you.

The real you is always the best you.

It takes real courage, but is the only way for complete fulfillment.

Things change and so can you—

A positive and powerful affirmation to live by.

Your desire to do something will allow
you to become something.

Opportunities arise when you add desire to your vision.

Success is not by chance, but taking one.

The more chances, the more opportunities.

Small minds judge many.

Ignorance leads to more ignorance.

With a vision comes happiness.

Dictate that vision in great detail,
and the world will respond.

Hate is a seed of disease that sprouts with thought.

Plants will die without water, just as
hate will do without thought.

What you feel becomes real.

Use this amazing power as an anchor for change.

Once you learn to forgive yourself, you'll forgive others.

Everything starts with you and the ability
to make that powerful choice.

Without love, you're dead—

Use these words as a mantra for a fulfilling life.

Be yourself in a world that wants to change you.

You can control your life, or life will control you.

With passion comes purpose.

Doing what you love will attract more of it.

When you forgive, you begin to live.

The world responds with open arms.

Your purpose is to find purpose.

Nothing will make you truly happy until
you find out why you're here.

Inspire those who fear with knowledge to persevere.

Be a shoulder to lean on, and offer
knowledge for them to move on.

Be the reason for someone to find happiness.

The simplest gesture creates an everlasting outcome.

Those who judge where you've been will
miss the greatness you're becoming.

Always separate yourself from these unforgiving souls.

Success is determined by your direct
belief of becoming successful.

The hardest decision is to know you're
worthy for such greatness.

You can't know everything, but you can become anything.

Success is not knowing it all, but doing it all.

Use what has shaped you to benefit you.

Dictate the scares, and transform them
into wisdom to move forward.

People will tell you what to do, but
follow your heart on how to do it.

Life rewards passion with direction.

Many will say you can't, but only you can say you can.

Their opinions are what they've
experienced in life and not yours.

Believe what you seek, as the same is seeking you.

Life denies nothing if you believe
you can become something.

Face your fears, or your fears will face you—

The hardest choice with the best rewards.

Having it all starts with the belief that you can.

Success starts as a mind-set and expands into a lifestyle.

Thanksgiving should not be a holiday, but a lifestyle.

A ritual you should master on this pathway to success.

You can change tomorrow by what you think about today.

Illustrate that amazing outcome every day
before you go to sleep at night.

The true power of self is no fear of being self.

Change hurts, but not changing will hurt more.

Stop worrying what people think, and start
being what you wish to become.

Focus on that person you see inside,
so it can manifest outside.

The smallest change can create the biggest rewards.

Dictate simple steps you could accomplish
daily, and everything will change for you.

Opposites attract nothing more than
future disappointments.

This theory I wish was taught to me,
as I learned it the hard way.

Your words today are a reflection of your tomorrow.

What you speak of, you bring of.

Everyone has faults, if that's what you're looking for.

You'll miss the gift of others if you only see one side.

It's amazing what others don't see until you stop doing it.

Do things because you want to, not because you have to.

You are your own problem, and indeed, the solution.

Illustrate what brings you down, and create
a list of what can bring you back up.

What you fear now, you could become later.

Fear is a powerful emotion, but still a chosen one.

We sometimes go through bad things that
inspire us to create great things.

There is a reason for everything,
and answers in everything.

Mean people have absolutely no meaning.

Stay away from those who want to use
you as their own punching bag.

A smile requires nothing but a choice.

Once you can master this spontaneous
behavior, it will change your life.

Ignorance creates more ignorance.

Learn from failure, and not keep doing
the same things that lead to failure.

Don't blame others, but learn from them.

Accept responsibility, and you'll find peace.

A blind mind will never allow the truth.

An open mind will always welcome the truth.

Your mind doesn't command you, but
takes commands from you.

The mind listens and proceeds to
manifest exactly what you tell it.

Children don't remember what you did for
them, but what you say to them.

Words will raise a child up or bring them down.

What you feel is a choice.

An emotion is brought to life by your choice to give it life.

Dwelling on your past will always limit your future.

Why dwell when you can always dream?

We never have a chance unless we
decide to give ourselves one.

You are worthy to create something
truly amazing if you decide to.

How you treat others is a direct reflection
of how you treat yourself.

True happiness starts within, and is projected out.

Blunt words have sharp edges.

The words you speak have a lasting effect on others.

When you love yourself, you heal yourself.

You are worthy to feel this inner peace of mind.

Believe that anything is possible, and
you create the impossible.

True faith in our abilities will always bring possibilities.

The world doesn't control your thoughts, only you do.

The world offer thoughts with things that happen, but you make the choice to live by it.

Lack is a mind-set. Abundance is a choice.

Dictate how you think, and see which
of these you focus on daily.

Don't focus on what troubles you, but what inspires you.

Things happen, but you can change that
with a vision for something better.

Always consider, there are more things
right with you than wrong.

This is essential for self-confidence and
will fuel the fire of passion for more.

Dreams die only by choice.

We're reminded everyday what we could become,
and our choice to be that reminder.

Be not who you have to be, but who you wish to be.

You will be so much happier when
you commit to this choice.

Challenges are there to help you, not hurt you.

Overcoming will always inspire your drive further.

The words you speak can bless you or destroy you.

Encourage yourself, so you don't destroy yourself.

Each day offers something to become something.

Everything changes when you become
observant to the world around you.

Just because someone called you something
doesn't mean you are that something.

Ignore the negative, as they mean nothing
to someone with a purpose.

Your obstacles can be opportunities.

An open mind will see opportunities in everything.

People don't understand you, because
they don't listen to you.

Don't explain, just be.

The best medicine is another who listens.

True friends always listen without judgment.

Depression can be described as someone who can't see the other side of life, even though it's right in front of them.

In your darkest times, know that you can overcome with a vision of greatness.

Following others will lead to a path to nowhere.

Lead your own life, and you won't have this problem.

Be your own light, not the shadow of others.

Standing behind people will only benefit them.

The tide will turn when you stop swimming against it.

Success will flow as smooth as a river once
you change your perception of it.

Every thought of the past is one less for the future.

Use your time well, as we are only here for a short period.

"Those who doubt will live without."

That simple rhyme should inspire you as a fact of life.

Consider obstacles as nothing more than inconveniences.

A great way to combat daily events.

Most say what they want, whereas achievers obtain what they want.

What category do you fall under with this?

Don't focus on what you don't have,
but what you can have.

It's all about how you think that will
determine your outcome.

Your future starts with illustrating one.

Write daily what you want, and the
world will help you get there.

Open minds offer creative solutions.

A mind of peace is always open.

The power of words can change a thought.
The power of thought can change a life.

Speak as you wish, and that wish will be granted.

Don't follow the path of others, but
create one so they follow you.

Followers will always be disappointed in their future.

Success is not denied by life, but how you think of life.

Life will always give you exactly what you put out.

We all have a past, but it doesn't
mean we need to live by it.

Live for the moment and not the memory.

We're not born to doubt, but taught to be that way.

Always follow what you feel, and trust
what you could become.

Surround yourself with those who
encourage you, not discourage you.

We all need a cheerleader besides ourselves.

You can never undo the past, but you
can always redo the future.

Every second forward is a chance to start anew.

Obstacles come and go, but dreams will always be there.

Beyond any obstacle is your dream waiting to happen.

Focus on what you want, not what you don't have.

Appreciate what you have, and give
thanks for what you wish to attain.

Consider everyday a chance instead of a struggle.

Getting through struggles are what gives you a chance.

Wisdom is gained by speaking less and listening more.

The more ignorance you show, the
more obstacles will come.

Hope looks at the obstacles. Faith overcomes them.

Faith offers courage, knowing you
have all you need to overcome.

Words of wisdom don't come from the mind, but the soul.

The deepest part of you will never forget powerful words.

Time for reflection creates an image for the future.

It's in the quiet time that we find who we are.

Our destiny will be defined by the
courage we put in front of it.

Courage determines and will create
possibilities for a better outcome.

Yesterday is a memory; today is a possibility.

Focus on the present which, by definition, is called a gift.

The consequence of ignorance is more ignorance.

The same path will be determined
by your inability to listen.

What you complain about now can be your reality later.

Speak your future by expressing gratefulness
to what you're dreaming it to be.

Think not of trials, but of triumphs.

You will progress much faster with a winning mind-set.

Beyond the negativity is a choice to live positively.

We are surrounded with it, but there is
the choice to live as you wish.

You don't find happiness, but only create it.

Few realize the amazing power we have to
create anything by focusing on it.

It is through the darkness that we can find happiness.

Darkness can never survive in a
mind looking for sunshine.

Change will hurt now, but not changing will hurt more.

Try to dictate what hurts, and describe in detail the life you wish without it.

You can't fight fear, but only face it.

Face all that hold you back.

When you change how you think, you
change who you become—

A simple fact of life worth your time to master.

What you speak more of, you'll get more of.

What you ask for in this world, you'll
get more of in this world.

With imagination, you create something from nothing.

Everything that you have was once imagination to attain.

You're not limited, unless you think that way.

To overcome anything is to believe
you can overcome anything.

The past is not your future, unless you decide for it to be.

Live in the moment that shapes your future,
rather than the past that will hurt it.

Others may judge, but only you know the truth.

Let others judge with ignorance, as you relax in peace.

Nothing is denied to those who believe.

What you believe is eventually what you receive.

What you're passionate about you brings about.

Passion adds fuel to what your heart truly desires.

When you allow yourself to trust again, you begin again.

Let it go!

Use karma as the gift you give yourself.

What good you do will always come back to you.

What you feel is what you become.

Every feeling is a seed you can't see, but will grow into something you can see.

A mind can never grow with small thinking.

Let your imagination run wild, and watch the magic.

Everything evolves around your perception of it.

What you feel about your surrounding will
bring more of those surroundings.

Be your own light, not the shadow of others.

Sunshine follows those who let it in.

With direction comes reason.

Every step forward will give you more reason to do so.

Failure starts from within.

It's what you believe in yourself that you become.

The body will always heal, but the
mind will always remember.

It's okay to remember, but damaging to dwell.

Be your own cause, and you'll be
rewarded by your own effects.

Cause is the starting point to everything by
which you receive the effect from that cause.

Dreams are the future delivered in advance.

Model Einstein and watch the unseen become seen.

Out from your storm is the power to create sunshine.

Storms won't last with a mind that expects sunshine.

We are blessed with something to help
others become something.

Believe the gifts you carry are essential
to help others in some way.

After the storm, there's always a rainbow.

You are the creator of that rainbow to move forward.

Do what you love to do, not what you have to do.

The world rewards love with more love.

The pain will stop when you decide to let it go.

Try to keep your focus on what you want to happen rather than on what has happened.

Just the thought of success brings you closer to it.

This is the starting point. The rest is up to you.

You never fail until you decide to.

Success is not denied unless you
believe you are being denied.

How you live now is what you create later.

Living is being something, and if what your being is what you want, then keep being that something.

Change may not be your choice, but it can be your path.

Things happen, but realize they can
be a blessing in disguise.

In the face of any downfall is the will to stand again.

You are blessed to overcome anything
when you truly believe you can.

Fear is a thought you bring to life.

Most important—fear is a chosen
thought you bring to life.

Time doesn't heal old wounds, only you can.

If you allow yourself the chance,
you'll give yourself a chance.

Change doesn't happen to you, but is created by you.

All change happens when you decide
to make change happen.

A thriving mind-set is denied nothing.

A thriving mind is imagination in motion.

What you choose to be ignorant of now
could come back to haunt you later.

Learn from your mistakes by learning from your mistakes.

It's being that person you wish to be now that creates the person you become later.

You make it happen by letting them happen.

You can't change who you are, but you can
change who you wish to become.

Accept who you are, and evolve even further from that.

Your eyes can see the world, but your
mind can see the future.

Imagination is a glimpse of your future reality.

We are not our past unless we decide to live by it.

Holding on to it will only bring more of it.

The past is not who you are, but who you were.

The past represents what you've been
through, not where you're going.

The pain of today can be your strength for tomorrow.

Pain creates wisdom which allows us to move
forward without creating more of it.

It may not make sense, but in time, will make sense.

Beyond what has happened is time to
heal from what has happened.

Failing forward is moving forward.

Failure is trying which allows you to learn
a better way to move forward.

Look to yourself with questions about yourself.

Always ask, and you'll always receive.

The meaning of words you speak now
will show its definition later.

What you speak of, you receive more of.

You attain exactly what you believe you can.

Your attitude can give you anything,
or take away everything.

If you can forgive others, you make room for others—

A powerful choice that leads to a positive outcome.

Lying doesn't solve problems but creates them.

The truth never needs explanation.

To win the game requires you to be your own coach.

If you can inspire yourself, you can change yourself.

It doesn't matter what you do, but it does where you stay.

Your environment today will have a direct
reflection of where you are tomorrow.

If you can get through the challenges,
you create possibilities.

A challenge is nothing more than an arrow
pointing in a different direction.

You have a choice to be something or become something.

We're already just being something, but it's our choice if we wish to become something.

Problems won't stay in a mind looking for solutions.

Open minds create positive outcomes.

Pain is temporary, but dwelling on it makes it permanent.

The more you think of, you bring of.

Focus on the solution, not the reason.

Focus not on what happened, but a
solution so it never happens again.

Every day you have a chance to do
something or become something.

Take a small step every day to become
what you truly wish to be.

What you're passionate about, you bring about.

Do what makes you happy and the world
responds by bringing you more of it.

Give yourself a future by not living in the past.

Learn from it, but don't dwell about it.

Life will change when you decide to change.

In that moment of choice, you bring
ideas to make it happen.

A goal is a dream in writing.

Be the author of your life.

Your history does not dictate your destiny.

ABOUT THE AUTHOR

Jerry Maldonado did not let the lack of a formal education hinder his love of words. From humble beginnings, he has penned three books, numerous columns, and interviewed many in the spotlight.

His words have been featured nationally and internationally with success stories that have inspired many to improve their own lives for the better.

With the release of this first book, Jerry has three more in production His diary-based books are a stepping-stone to help others manifest with the power of the pen, unlimited imagination, and the laws of the universe. You are your own creator of self. You set the guidelines and put forth powerful energy to manifest a beautiful outcome.

9 781640 287822